Coffee Talk

An Uncle and His Nephew
Discuss the Nature of Truth

By

J.R. Dickens

This story is a work of fiction, but it sure has a lot of truth in it. Any resemblance between the author and the character named "Uncle Bob" is probably coincidental—although it's true the author's middle name is *Robert* and he has been an uncle since the age of eight.

ISBN (Print Edition): 978-0-9992870-0-2

ISBN (Kindle Edition): 978-0-9992870-5-7

Introduction

As I put the finishing touches on this short book (written over a long Fourth-of-July weekend), I'm inclined to describe it as a step toward recovering the lost art of intellectual discourse in an age of social media overload—when our "friends" are numbered in the hundreds and our personal interactions are measured in fractions of a second. We have all become like ships passing in the night, and in many cases, having no idea where anyone is really going.

When I was a kid I remember my parents spending lots of table time with neighbors over a pot of coffee. (This was back in the early 1970s—in a quiet suburb outside of Houston.) Even today, coffee has magical powers to lubricate the most challenging social interactions if we allow it to. The act of simply sharing a pot of coffee can help two people find enough common ground to talk—and if we can keep the conversation going, we might just find a few more things we have in common besides a taste for that bitter black brew. (Personally, I prefer a light roast, with heavy cream and a generous scoop of sweetener, in case you're planning to invite me over sometime.)

The conversation in this book delves into some difficult concepts, so you may find it helpful to refer to the Glossary from time to time (glossary terms are indicated in **boldface** when they first appear in the text). I have also included a number of questions that can be used for personal review and/or group study.

I hope you enjoy reading the book as much as I have enjoyed writing it for you.

J.R. Dickens
Woodland Park, Colorado

Chapter 1

It's a sunny Saturday morning in your new neighborhood—just the kind of morning to take a walk around the block and say hello to some of your new neighbors. So far, they all seem quite friendly and have made you feel right at home in your new house.

You are in a bit of a rush as you head out the door. Your uncle will be stopping by in a little while to see how you're settling in.

Stepping out into the fresh air, you walk down the path to the sidewalk, utterly settled in your conviction that in this old world of ours, *up is up* and *down is down*. Not a doubt in your mind.

The first person you encounter lives right next door. John waves and smiles as he calls out, "Up is up and down is down!" Of course it is!

Walking a bit further, you greet your neighbor Nancy who waves and calls out, "Up is down and down is up!" Wait. *What*?

Before you turn the corner of the next block, your neighbor Mike appears from behind his bushy hedge and calls out, "Up is right and down is left!" Whoa. *Really*?

As you are beginning to ponder the perplexities of what you've heard, most of it against your own convictions, you look across the street in time to see your neighbor Joanne step out of her front door with the dog in tow and greet you with a hearty, "Up is left and down is right!"

Moments later as you're about to cross a busy intersection, your neighbor Christopher whizzes around the corner on his ten-speed bike and says, "Up is front and down is back!"

Stunned by this new revelation, you take a few more steps before you come upon your neighbor Michelle, who from behind her baby's stroller waves and calls out, "Up is back and down is front!"

As you round the last corner and finally catch a glimpse of your front steps, your neighbor George waves and declares, "Up is green and down is blue!"

With such a bewildering assortment of ideas in your mind, you've never been happier to get home.

Now as you take a deep breath and relax in front of the TV, your favorite newscaster intones with utmost certainty, "This just in. Numerous reliable sources confirm that up is up *and* down is up. Tune in to the evening broadcast for the latest developments."

At this point, you're beginning to wonder if it's even possible to make sense of anything you've heard. Everyone thinks he is right—

but they all can't be right at the same time, can they? Or maybe nobody is ever really "right" or "wrong." There's just perspective, some might say, and therefore everyone sees the world in a different way. Through his own set of lenses, figuratively speaking.

Just as the fog of confusion and despair is rolling back into your mind, you're suddenly startled by a hard rap on the front door. Fearing that one of the neighbors is about to compound your raging doubts, you're relieved to discover that it's Uncle Bob who's just arrived. Should you tell him what just happened? Does it even matter?

After offering your uncle a cup of coffee—and preparing one for yourself as well—the two of you sit down at the kitchen table to chat. Uncle senses your concerned state of mind.

"What seems to be bothering you this morning?"

"You wouldn't believe me if I told you."

Uncle leans forward with both hands on his coffee cup. "Try me. I'm all ears."

After a sigh and a long pause, you slowly begin to relate the bizarre events of the morning. Frankly, some of it is already a little fuzzy, but you recall enough of the detail to explain your sense of despair.

Uncle hasn't moved a muscle. After a moment of reflection he says, "Hmm," and takes a noisy sip of hot coffee. The cup lands back on the table with a gentle thud that sounds like the rap of a gavel signaling that court is now in session. Uncle then states matter-of-factly, "You're not sure what to believe."

"I'm not sure I can believe *anything* anymore." The fog of despair seems to be growing heavier.

Chapter 2

Uncle attempts to cut through the fog. "I perceive that your sour mood is the result of a bad case of **cognitive dissonance**."

You barely hear Uncle's comment, but the funny expression he just used has roused you somewhat like a distant foghorn echoing across the still water.

"Huh?"

"*Cognitive dissonance*," he repeats for dramatic effect. But you already knew the phrase was designed to arouse your interest. Uncle likes to do that sort of thing. "It means that your mind has been presented with an assortment of conflicting claims. Your sense of despair results from an inability to reconcile everything you've heard."

The fog begins to thin a bit as you realize that Uncle actually might understand what's bothering you.

"When you started out on your walk this morning, there was no confusion in your mind. You already believed with certainty that *up is up*, and *down is down*. John's comment reinforced your belief. But Nancy contradicted it. And then all the other assorted views of *up* and *down* added to your confusion."

Uncle was right. And that's where he found you a few minutes ago—slumped in a living room chair in the throes of despair.

Uncle finishes his thought as you continue to ponder your miserable condition. "Now your certainty has been demolished and you're afraid you'll never get it back."

If only he knew. Or did he?

"You already have part of the answer," he says, as if it were that simple. Uncle could be annoying in that way. At the very moment you're convinced he's understanding your problem, he says something that proves he's not tracking with you at all.

"How could I possibly have part of the answer when I have nothing but a collection of confusing and conflicting information?"

"It's logical," he says, again in a matter-of-fact way that suggests that anyone could see precisely what he meant. He raises his cup and drains the last of the coffee. "Do you mind if I get another cup?"

At moments like this you wonder whether the two of you are even having the same conversation.

After refilling his coffee cup, Uncle sits back down at the kitchen table and breaks the silence. The pause in the conversation has focused your attention to such a degree that you hardly notice the last of the lingering fog.

Leaning forward, Uncle goes on: "What you're experiencing is either a **paradox** or a **contradiction**. Or maybe a little of each."

You've heard the words before, but don't they mean the same thing?

"A contradiction," he says, "is when two or more statements cannot be true at the same time and in the same way. A paradox is when things that *appear* to be in contradiction are not. A paradox is usually resolved with additional information. That means you have to find the missing pieces."

You decide that maybe you're going to need another cup of coffee, as well.

Chapter 3

As you fill your cup with the last of the coffee, Uncle continues.

"Let's start with the contradiction. You say the world is round. I say the world is flat. We can't both be right at the same time and in the same way. If the world is round, it isn't flat—and vice versa."

After you take your place back at the table, you allow Uncle's point to sink in. It's now your turn to speak. After a moment you add, "One of us has to be wrong."

"That's one possibility. What is the other?" Uncle looks at you intently, waiting for you to think it through.

"Or we're both wrong."

"Of course! Now you understand what's called the **law of noncontradiction**." Uncle beams. He's taking you on a journey of discovery, and it seems to be going better than your walk around the block. But there's another moment of silence. He's waiting for you to apply what you just learned.

"When I took my walk this morning I was already sure that *up is up* and *down is down*. But after talking to everyone along the way, and hearing so many ideas that were different from mine, I could no longer be sure."

Uncle leans back in his chair and takes the measure of his nephew. "Go on."

"It's possible that I was wrong, and that one of my friends is right. But it's also possible that we're all wrong."

Uncle sips his coffee and brings the cup in for a soft landing this time, then resumes the didactic glare. There's something more he wants you to understand.

"I suppose it's possible that two of us could be right, but we don't have enough information to see it."

With another sip of coffee, Uncle adds, "That's called a paradox."

"And if we're going to resolve the paradox, we need a way to find the missing information."

Uncle nods. "Talking helps. And asking questions. *Good* questions. The kind that get to the heart of a matter."

You're pretty sure Uncle just said you don't ask good questions. Sensing your discomfort, he adds, "We have to rekindle our sense of wonder and curiosity. It's almost that simple. When we're having a conversation, we have a tendency to take too much for granted."

At times like this you feel like a child playing chess with a grand master, but in Uncle's case you know he isn't trying to beat you, he's trying to lead you. He wants to teach you. And he's not inclined to simply give you the answer to a question—he's going to give you a way to ask and answer your own questions.

Chapter 4

At that very moment you begin to feel the fog rolling back in. There is a new source of doubt that is suddenly trying to take hold.

"What if there is no ultimate truth, and everything is just relative? Don't some people say that everyone has his own truth?"

Uncle leans back again. "Perhaps it's time to talk about **equivocation**, since it will also help us understand the nature of the paradox."

The chess master is making another strong move. Where is he going this time? Your fog of doubt is now reverting back to a fog of confusion!

Uncle pauses again, letting the statement sink in as he chooses his next words.

"Whenever we're having a conversation, definitions are key. You're right that some people say 'truth is relative,' and such a belief has important implications for communication. It's possible for two people to be using the same words in a conversation, but using them to mean different things. We have to ask what people *mean* by what they *say*."

It makes sense. You reply, "If we're using the same words in different ways, we won't understand each other."

Uncle looks up from his coffee cup with another hard stare. "And?"

"We'll get frustrated—maybe even angry—when the other person doesn't seem to understand our point. We'll be talking past each other without realizing it. And emotions will start to take over."

"It's called **emotional hijacking**. That's one of the dangers of equivocation. It may seem tedious to you that I spend a lot of effort to define words, but if we don't have the same definitions, we're using the same-sounding words, but speaking different languages."

"And that only adds to the confusion," you say, as if to complete Uncle's sentence. Just as he intended.

"Now let's take another look at how equivocation confuses things. The relativist says 'truth is relative,' but how can that be a true statement?"

Now you're feeling lost again. Uncle has a way of pushing you as far as you can go. This time he sees that you're struggling and takes the nonverbal cue to answer his own question. But just as he begins to speak, Uncle sees that you're jolted by a flash of insight and he pauses again.

The question rolls off your tongue. "How can the relativist think that he's making a true statement when his statement is claiming there is no truth?"

A slight smile creeps over Uncle's face. He waits again, so there must be more.

You speak again. "He's breaking the law of. . ."

"*Noncontradiction.*" Uncle completes the statement as if he were reading your mind. "Or else he's using the word 'truth' to mean different things when he says, 'truth is relative' but at the same time he wants you to believe that he is making a 'true' statement."

Now he goes on: "There are a couple of possibilities regarding the relativist's statement. One is that for the statement to be true, it must violate the **laws of logic**. But if there is no truth, there is no logic. The other possibility is that the relativist is engaging in equivocation. He's either changing the meaning of the word 'truth' or he's changing the meaning of the word 'relative.' Truth is true *by definition*. Truth can never be relative."

"Unless you're a relativist, in which case, 'truth' can mean whatever you want it to."

"Which means, of course, that it's no longer truth."

Although you are have some difficulty digesting the new lesson, something else occurs to you that seems to be an important point from just a moment ago.

"Uncle, if truth is relative, how could we have a conversation? Even words would be meaningless."

Rather than responding to your question, he waits for you to answer it yourself.

"The relativist is contradicting himself by trying to use words to make the claim that **relativism** is true."

Another long stare.

"He can't live consistently with his own belief system."

Uncle nods and smiles ever so slightly. He is visibly pleased that you are beginning to see how to think about the kind of truth claims you heard on the sidewalk this morning. You don't have all the answers yet, but this seems like a good start.

Chapter 5

"You're discovering one of the most important principles of good **philosophy**. In order for a belief system to have intellectual credibility, it must be logically consistent."

This is the first moment it occurs to you that you've been talking about philosophy all morning.

"But don't we first have to make an assumption that *logic* is true?"

"Indeed. The assumption is called an **axiom**. We can't prove that it's true, but if it isn't, we can't prove anything."

Your head is starting to spin again. There are layers of complexity here that you're struggling to latch onto.

Uncle continues. "Here's an easy way to sum up the problem with relativism: In order to believe it, you'd have to reject both **rationality** and **objectivity**."

Good grief. More big words. Uncle sees the pained expression on your face—as if you are on the verge of brain overload.

"Rationality is just what we've been talking about—following the laws of logic. And anything we call a 'law' has to be objectively true. It's what we call a **universal**. Objectivity means something is always true whether we choose to believe it or not. Objective truth is outside of us." Uncle pauses a bit to let the words sink in. "Take this kitchen table. Either it's real or it's imaginary. If it's imaginary, then we have to imagine it or else it's not here. If it's real, it doesn't matter whether we imagine it to be real or not. It's *really* here." Uncle makes a fist and pounds on the table for dramatic effect. The coffee cups rattle and a bit of coffee splatters onto the table top.

You're pretty sure you're following the argument. "So the relativist would say the table isn't real?"

"Correct. The relativist would say that you and I only *imagine* it to be real. We only imagine we're leaning against it, and we only imagine we're resting our coffee cups on it."

"The coffee cups aren't real either."

"Only to the extent we think they are real."

"Uncle, that sounds like nonsense."

"That's a polite way to put it. Now, think about what happens when we try to claim that *all* truth is relative."

"I'm stumped! In that case, how would it be possible to know anything at all?"

"Good question! That's precisely the point. It wouldn't. Just as logic is dead at the doorstep of relativism, so is knowledge. Anything we *claim* to know could never be known for sure—even our very own existence. One person says one thing, and another person says another. Both claim to be speaking the truth. And if we follow the argument all the way back around, we're forced to ask the question: 'How do we know that relativism is true?'"

You finish Uncle's thought. "Relativism caves in on itself. If it's true, it must be false."

Uncle pounds the table again, this time with a sense of jubilation. Cups rattle and coffee splatters.

Things are starting to make more sense, but frankly, you're still overwhelmed by all the philosophy that Uncle is throwing at you. But he's hardly done.

"In the world of philosophy we have a concept called **epistemology**. It's the **science** of knowledge. It's the answer to the question, 'How do we know what we know?' And it has never been a trivial question for philosophers to wrestle with. If we can't answer the challenge of epistemology, we can't get out of the starting gate. Logic is dead. Knowledge is dead. Philosophy is dead. So you can understand why epistemology is such an important part of philosophy."

Your wheels are grinding, but they're still turning in spite of the internal resistance. Slowly but surely. "Uncle, what happens to science if relativism is true?"

Uncle is watching you as if to peer into your thoughts, and he has already anticipated the question. "The **scientific method** is designed to help us discover objective truth about the universe we live in. If there is no truth outside the human mind, scientific inquiry is just an illusion. There is nothing 'out there' to discover."

Your wheels continue to turn, a bit faster now, but still grinding with the effort. "What point is there in trying to understand the universe if we can't learn anything about it anyway? Would there be any point to scientific progress?"

"None at all. You've now brought us to the next important philosophical question. It's called **teleology**. We'll talk about it after lunch. I can see you're ready for an extended break."

You take Uncle's measure and offer, "How do you feel about ham and cheese?"

"On wheat?"

You push back from the table with the word "teleology" still ringing in your ears. You had no idea you were guiding the conversation so skillfully.

Chapter 6

The lunch break came at a good time. Your mind was starting to tire after wrestling with some difficult questions all morning. Uncle is an interesting fellow to talk to, but he can be positively exhausting. To your relief, the two of you make small talk over lunch so your mind has time to rest a bit. Uncle plays along but seems a little bored.

Since knocking on the door this morning, Uncle has thrown an entire dictionary of philosophy at you. But you can see that the words are illustrating important concepts that you've only wondered about from time to time—things that would never have occurred to you on your walk this morning. And now you're suddenly immersed in them, and trying not to drown.

What was that strange word Uncle used right before lunch?

Uncle plops down in the living room chair and meets your gaze across the coffee table. He is visibly energized after the ham sandwich, and he picks up right where he left off an hour ago.

"Quick review. Epistemology is the science that tells us we're really here. As Descartes expressed it famously, '*Cogito ergo sum*—I think, therefore I am.' He proved his own existence by thinking about it. Sounds silly, but it's actually quite profound. Now teleology is the science that wants to understand our purpose. *Why* we are here."

Teleology. That was the word. For a moment it occurs to you that maybe you should have been taking some notes this morning.

"Back to your excellent question about science. When we bring epistemology and teleology together, it gives us the basis for doing science—the existence of discoverable knowledge—and it gives us a reason to be curious about the universe we live in. If our lives had no purpose, then it really wouldn't matter whether we learned anything or not."

Without thinking at all, you blurt, "We might as well jump off a cliff." Now you feel stupid for saying it and start to blush. Uncle senses your embarrassment, but he was leading you right to the conclusion.

"Without realizing it, you just used an argumentative device called the **reductio ad absurdum**. You've taken an idea to its logical conclusion in order to show that it's absurd."

At this point you're not even sure what language Uncle is speaking. Maybe he's been watching too much *Harry Potter*. He continues.

"The state of modern philosophy is such a mess that some say suicide is the only important question we have left to address. I kid you not. So you have no reason to feel badly. This is where the question naturally leads."

You regain your composure and push on. "But Uncle, it can't be true. We have to have a purpose."

"I happen to agree with you. But there's a school of thought that says we have no purpose because we're the byproduct of pure chance in an old and chaotic universe. We just have the existential misfortune of being a sufficiently advanced intelligence—unlike any before us—that can think about the fact that our lives are meaningless."

"Along with everything else." The conversation is suddenly flowing like a tennis match.

"Yes. In a purposeless universe, *everything* is meaningless by definition. But something inside the human heart finds it necessary to assign meaning to our lives, even if we have no good reason to do so. The alternative—as we've seen—is despair and suicide."

"But you don't believe that."

Uncle chuckles. "Of course not! To believe that our existence resulted from pure chance is as absurd as believing that truth is relative."

You parry. "Don't scientists tell us the universe created itself? Or that there are millions of universes, and ours is the one that happened to produce intelligent life?"

"Of course. They have to say something to explain the obvious fact that we're here. No less a scientist than Dr. Stephen Hawking asserted the **self-creation** narrative. But can you see what is wrong with popular claims like the ones you mentioned?"

"Self-creation and **multiverse** theories can't be proven, can they?"

"They cannot. By the way, you're following the argument quite well at this point, so there's no need to hedge your bets by posing the answer as a question. But to be more precise, the scientific method works on the basis of proposing a theory—an **hypothesis**—and then collecting evidence to *disprove* it. Science doesn't 'prove' any of its theories. That's not how science works."

The conversation is moving so quickly at this point that you're starting to get a bit anxious—somewhat like a downhill skier who's picking up so much speed on a steep run that he's afraid he won't be able to stop. "Hang on. I don't think I'm following what you just said."

"No problem. Let's take a quick breather. Do you mind if I make some fresh coffee?"

"Of course. I mean, of course *not*. Please help yourself." You're glad Uncle is offering to make the coffee himself so you can clear your mind.

Uncle pushes himself out of the comfy chair and strolls into the kitchen. He returns a few minutes later as the sounds and scents of brewing coffee drift into the living room.

After returning to his chair, Uncle pauses before continuing, and makes a point to slow his cadence a bit.

"Let's think about what science can do. First, notice that science is an unfolding story. It's a slow, methodical discovery of new information, sometimes piece by tiny piece. Meticulous, even tedious. Science never knows all there is to know, nor can it ever know. And a little later we'll talk about some things that science can never discover—the

33

kinds of knowledge that must come from someplace *besides* science. But science is pretty good at what it does—make observations, propose theories, and disprove its theories with data."

You fidget in the chair even though it's quite comfortable. Even at a slower pace, Uncle is getting harder to follow—but he can see your puzzled expression and pauses once again to let you ask a question.

"I'm confused. I was under the impression that our scientific knowledge is growing by leaps and bounds. We live in an age of rapid technological progress, don't we?"

"Without a doubt. However, it's only easy to see how much we know—or how little—by looking backward. Any age can seem advanced in relation to the past. But anything we know at any point in history is a mere fraction of the discoverable knowledge of the universe."

"So we never really know what we *don't* know?"

"In reality, science has to operate on a very small amount of data. And one of the hardest parts of being a scientist is that you can never know how much you *don't* know at any given point in time. In fact, scientists can easily be fooled by what they *do* know."

Your mind is starting to catch up with the flow of the conversation again. "And that's why you say science can never 'prove' its theories?"

"Correct. So we devise our theories in a way that makes them easy to disprove with just a little data. In other words, we make our theories *falsifiable*."

"And that helps explain why theories in science change so much. We find some data or run some experiments and the results don't fit the theory."

"Precisely. I like to say that we can measure the progress of science on the basis of how many theories we discard. New data gives us new knowledge that requires better theories to explain what we see. Theory has to accommodate the facts, not the other way around."

"Okay, I'm tracking with your explanation, but we were talking about purpose. Tee—lee—*what*?" The word just doesn't seem to stick in your mind no matter how many times you hear it.

"Teleology. If the universe is an accident—along with everything in it—then we have no purpose. And what are the explanations of origins we hear from science?"

"Self-creation and multiverse. But wait. Neither one is the kind of theory that science can test!"

"Quite right. They are in the realm of axioms that must be assumed because they cannot be proved."

"Or disproved. But self-creation doesn't even make sense. Nothing creates itself. And multiverse is pure imagination. Nobody has seen a multiverse."

"Nor a '**Big Bang**' for that matter." Sensing a high point in the discussion, Uncle tees up the final shot. "So if the 'scientific' explanation of origins is *unscientific.* . . ."

Without missing a beat, you finish his thought. "Then we're all operating in the realm of religious beliefs."

Uncle flashes a broad smile. "And unfortunately, scientists often fail to make a distinction between what they know from science and what they merely assert as an article of faith." After another dramatic pause he exclaims, "I think the coffee's ready."

Chapter 7

The break in the conversation gives you an opportunity to digest the last hour of rapid-fire discussion as you stir some cream and sugar into your coffee. You're not sure where it's all leading, but you're learning quite a bit and enjoying the stimulating company.

Uncle quietly makes his own coffee, leaving you to your thoughts for a few minutes. The intensity of the conversation is a bit like a fast-break basketball game that requires frequent time-outs so the players can catch a breather. Except that it's obvious Uncle doesn't need the break. He's watching *you* sprint up and down the court.

As the two of you take your seats in the living room, Uncle begins again, somewhat more reservedly. "Science likes to portray itself as objective and empirical—in a Joe Friday, 'just the facts' kind of way—in stark contrast to the religious types who rely on the biases of ancient mythology and blind faith." He waits for you to rejoin the flow of the discussion.

"Meaning, religious types like *you*?"

Uncle takes the cue to continue. "I'm a bit of an oddball as both a scientist and a 'religious type.' But the irony is that the secular scientist is every bit as religious even though he doesn't realize it. Probably because scientists aren't particularly adept at philosophy. They don't have to think about their **presuppositions**, so they don't."

Uncle is reminding you that it's hard for you to remember exactly what his PhD was about. Engineering, you think. Something like that. But when you sit down to talk to him, he sounds like someone who's almost as fluent as a scientist and a philosopher and a theologian.

Uncle allows you time to think through his statement. After a moment you ask, "Would it be fair to say that scientists place a lot of faith in their science?"

"That's a very astute question. They do because they *must*. Otherwise they would not be able to do science at all. Frankly, it takes a number of very important assumptions in order to do science. Mathematical laws, for instance. Logic. **Causality**. **Induction**. **Uniformity**. All of which are **metaphysical**—meaning, outside the realm of things we can see and touch. Outside the realm of empirical science. Axioms."

Uncle is on a roll and rapidly building up a head of steam. At this point you're in danger of getting hopelessly lost, so you execute an evasive maneuver. "Earlier you said that science can't answer certain questions. What did you mean by that?"

Uncle nods. "Thank you for bringing us back to that question. Here's a simple way to think about it: Science is the kind of endeavor that can tell us what is *possible*, but it can't give purpose to our actions, and it can't tell us the difference between right and wrong."

The pause is your cue to connect the dots again. Uncle reaches for his mug on the coffee table. It's his polite way of giving you extra time to reply.

"So science needs *tee-lee* . . . teleology to have a reason to do science. We talked about that part. But what about right and wrong?"

Uncle takes a sip of coffee and places the cup back on the table. "This is the branch of philosophy called **ethics**. And for all intents and purposes, both teleology and ethics are purely religious matters."

"Because you can't test them in a laboratory?"

"You have the right idea. Think about running a clinical trial for a new prescription drug. Science can set up an experiment and observe the outcomes—which patients got better, which got worse, which weren't helped—but it can't tell us *why* we should care about making people better with medicine, or whether it's better for someone to live or die."

"We're back to the cliff." Before finishing the morbid thought, you bite your tongue and start to blush again.

Uncle fixes his gaze at you. "Go on."

"Well, medicine is *supposed* to be about helping people, but without knowing right and wrong, you could help people get better with a drug that cures their illness, or you could just throw them off a cliff."

Uncle chuckles at the graphic hyperbole. He knows you're saying it to be provocative. But he also knows it's precisely the kind of ethical question we have to answer.

You finish your line of inquiry. "How do we figure out the difference between right and wrong? It seems as though we are always changing our minds about that question."

Uncle flashes another brief smile as he reaches for the coffee cup again.

Chapter 8

With his elbows on the armrests, Uncle is still holding the coffee cup in front of his face with both hands as if he is about to take another sip. "There are two basic schools of thought in the world of ethics: **deontology** and **consequentialism**."

Whap! You feel like you've just been smacked with the philosophy dictionary again. Every time it stings a little longer. Now you *really* wish you'd been taking notes.

Uncle quickly senses your despair. "Not to worry. We'll take it one step at a time. Let's start with the one that is almost self-explanatory—consequentialism."

Self-explanatory! Since when have big words like this ever been self-explanatory?

"The question is, 'On what basis do we make moral choices?' One way is by looking at the *consequences* of our choices, and deciding what is 'right' and 'wrong' based on the results produced by each possible choice. Hence, consequentialism. The most well-know consequential ethic is called **utilitarianism**."

Whap again. This is turning into a linguistic nightmare.

Uncle resumes. "Utilitarianism is also somewhat self-explanatory. It tells us that the 'right' choice is the one that maximizes the *utility* of all those affected by the decision. We sometimes say that the goal is to maximize satisfaction or happiness."

"You mean something like 'the most good for the most people'—that kind of an idea?"

After noticing the exasperation on your face a few minutes ago, Uncle is encouraged to see that you're tracking with the discussion. "Yes, that's another way to describe it." And then uncharacteristically, Uncle asks you a direct question: "How would you critique that kind of an ethical system?"

The question catches you off guard, but oddly enough, you were already thinking about the answer. "Well, for one thing, how can we ever really know what constitutes the most good?"

Uncle leans forward in his chair, pleased by your insight. "Yes, that's a very good observation. There's much more we could add, but let's move on for now."

You're still thinking about utilitarianism—what a word!—but Uncle has other plans for the conversation.

"The other broad category of ethical philosophy is deontology. It means following a set of rules or duties. In the deontological system of ethics, you only look at *choices*, not consequences." Uncle pauses a beat, then asks another direct question. "How does that kind of system strike you?"

"Well, it seems as though following the rules would be simpler than trying to guess at the outcomes. But where do the rules come from?"

Uncle unexpectedly breaks into a hearty laugh. "Outstanding observation! If we were to continue the critique of both deontology and consequentialism, we'd still have to eventually grapple with the million-dollar question." Uncle pauses, this time for dramatic effect. "*'Who says?'*—in other words, who or what is the moral authority behind the rules?"

You can only hope Uncle is asking rhetorical questions, because you certainly don't have any answers. Philosophy is starting to feel like a bottomless pit. You wonder whether *anybody* can answer questions like these. Haven't philosophers been arguing about it for thousands of years?

Uncle's next words are like the sound of the school bell to your ears. "Let's take ten. We've covered a lot of ground."

Chapter 9

Your head is still spinning after digesting the most recent flurry of philosophical vocabulary. Uncle certainly has a thing for big words. And big concepts. The stretch break came just in time to spare you from tripping an assortment of mental circuit breakers. The two of you are now settling back into the living room chairs as the afternoon shadows grow longer.

Uncle begins. "I could tell that you were struggling with the discussion on ethical philosophy. But let's bring it back to the world of science. What have we learned?" Uncle leans back in the armchair and sips from a fresh cup of coffee as you collect your thoughts.

"You took us through an overview of ethics to explain why science can't answer ethical questions. But I think I may have gotten a bit lost on the way."

Uncle chuckles again. He's not laughing *at* you—he knows he's challenging you to think in a new way, and you're actually keeping up quite well.

"Knowing that you're confused is part of the learning process. It's part of the struggle to understand, like a hard workout that pushes you to the limits of your physical abilities. But compare the way you feel now to the feeling you had earlier this morning. You were confused, but in a futile, despairing kind of way—worried that you'd never find a way out of the confusion. That you'd never get answers. That you were permanently stuck in a state of cognitive dissonance where nothing made any sense."

"Is it my imagination that most of the world can't even begin to sort out the confusion? Like my neighbors?"

"It's not your imagination. If you're operating from a relativistic **worldview**—as most people are these days—there are no ultimate answers, only the vague certitude of personal opinions. It's getting harder and harder to find people who know how to think critically about what they claim to believe."

"Which may explain why everyone I talked to this morning had a different idea about something as obvious as *up* and *down*."

Uncle nods. "Yes. Each one of your neighbors—and the talking heads on TV as well—each one of them carries a strongly held opinion that most likely is not supported by the evidence of argumentation. In other words, they may be able to clearly state their beliefs with great conviction, but they will be unable to defend those beliefs when challenged to offer proof."

"And if I'm following your point, there's a big difference between opinion and proof."

"All the difference. As one of my favorite Christian teachers explains it succinctly, 'Opinions have no argumentative weight.' Which means it's one thing to have an opinion, and quite another to have a good reason for it."

"And isn't that why people just seem to talk past each other?"

"Much of the public discourse involves people taking one side or another on an issue, drawing a hard line in between, and then shouting at the other side. Not very productive when it comes to understanding our differences."

"You said something about 'proofs.' What does that refer to?"

"Good question. Generally, we can talk about logical proofs or objective proofs. One can offer a logical argument for a certain belief—what we call a **syllogism**—or one can offer objective evidence for a belief. Facts and data."

Syllogism. Ack! Another philosophy word. "And you said this morning that the problem with relativism is. . . ." Your words trail off as you try to recall exactly what Uncle said.

"That logic and objectivity are both dead at the doorstep of relativism. There can be neither logical nor objective proofs to support an idea in a relativistic system. In other words," once again pausing for dramatic effect, "relativism *proves* nothing and *refutes* nothing. It is—as I like to put it—philosophically bankrupt. Think of it as man's philosophy hitting rock bottom."

You sit back and take a deep breath at this point. Uncle pauses again as the words sink in. It's a little stunning, actually. *Relativism proves nothing?*

Uncle adds a final thought. "If relativism is true, then it has no content whatsoever. As a relativist, you could believe anything or nothing. Relativism is quite possibly the most absurd philosophy ever invented. It excludes nothing."

You're not quite sure you understand what Uncle meant by that last statement. "'Relativism excludes nothing.' Can you help me with that?"

"Sure." Uncle slows his cadence once again so you have time to catch up. "One way to know what's in a philosophical system is to look at what it excludes. Atheism excludes the belief in God, and vice versa. I can't be an atheist and a theist at the same time. Relativism doesn't have the tools of rationality or objectivity to explain either what it includes or what it excludes. When it comes to relativism, anything goes. Absolutely any-thing. No one can ever really be 'wrong.'"

You're not quite sure how the explanation is useful, but regaining your composure, you redirect: "So relativism is going to be useless when it comes to answering ethical ques-tions?"

"Completely. And that's partly the point of it. Many relativists are deliberately trying to avoid moral responsibility. They are seeking what I call '**radical autonomy**'—the idea that no one, anywhere, can ever tell them how to live their lives."

Uncle has struck a chord. You ponder the statement before responding. "Honestly, I don't like being told what to do, either—so I can see the appeal of that idea. But how does it work out in the real world?"

"Simple. It's impossible. Radical auton-omy is anarchy. No rules. No social structure whatsoever, because social structures inevitably place *limits* on what the individuals in society can do."

"Then what happens to something like the family?"

"Family is the first casualty because family life introduces the specter of taking individual responsibility—first for yourself, then for the members of your family. Family requires *self-sacrifice*—a willingness to subdue your own selfish desires in order to serve the needs of others. Family is therefore **antithetical**—one could even say *hostile*—to personal autonomy."

"And without social structures, it would be 'every man for himself'?"

"Yes, exactly. What kind of a world would that be?"

"In a word? I think it would be brutal. No restraint on individual behavior? And what about my individual rights?"

"You'd have no rights, except the 'right' to do whatever you want in relation to anyone else. Anarchy is a world without duty *or* responsibility. It would reduce our existence to Darwin's ethic of **'survival of the fittest**.' It's the law of the jungle. And it would be far more violent than anything we see in the world today."

"That's actually a terrifying prospect."

"It is. And it shows that our individual beliefs about things like personal autonomy have huge consequences for society as a whole."

"If I understood you correctly, you said that anarchy is impossible. Why couldn't we have the 'Wild West frontier' kind of society?"

"Anarchy is an unstable system. Every system seeks equilibrium. And the equilibrium that emerges from anarchy is tyranny.

The one who is able, by force, to exercise authority over another is certainly going to do so."

As if to complete his thought, you add, "And that might be even worse than anarchy."

"Arguably, yes. But only if you had a moral framework that could make those kinds of value judgments."

"But wasn't the point of autonomy to avoid being under someone else's authority?"

"Ironic, isn't it? Anarchy inevitably leads to despotism. Most of us—except for those who are part of the privileged ruling class—would end up as slaves. Or cannon fodder. Plenty of historical precedent for both outcomes."

You're still alarmed by the images of a world detached from a benevolent social order (including family) as you circle back to the question Uncle posed earlier in the conversation. "If man does not make law for himself, where does the law come from? Who has the moral authority to make law?"

Uncle grins. "You have to go to the source of the law, of course."

Chapter 10

"One of the most amusing ironies of relativism," Uncle begins, "is that you'll never meet anyone who really believes it. Someone might claim, on the one hand, that there is no moral law constraining his behavior (or anyone else's, if they're consistent). But you will always find the professed relativist to have an assortment of moral hot buttons."

You're a bit surprised by Uncle's observation. "What do you mean by 'moral hot buttons'?"

"For instance, personal or social causes that the relativist cares about. Things he thinks are important, and he thinks you should agree with him. Take slavery, for example. Does slavery matter in a relativistic world? In a word, *no*—because *nothing* matters, not even one human enslaving and mistreating another. In the world of the relativist, anything a man *can* do is 'okay.' Anything. There are no moral constraints. And yet," as Uncle turns his attention back to the coffee mug on the table, "humans seem to have an innate sense of right and wrong. A sense of justice and fairness, of cruelty and evil. A moral nature that is not reflected anywhere in the animal kingdom."

Uncle lifts the cup and takes a sip. He leaves his last statement hanging, like a curveball over the middle of the plate. Now it's your job to clobber it. "Where does man get this innate sense of morality?"

"The answer depends on whom you ask. The atheist, for example, believes that man evolved from the slime, and somewhere along the long and brutal evolutionary chain of development, he learned that his chances for survival were improved by cooperation with his knuckle-dragging brethren."

"So the evolutionist would say morality is just adaptive behavior that fits the framework of survival. But that wouldn't make an apparently moral choice a moral *requirement*, would it?"

"Quite insightful of you to make that connection. I would put it this way: in the absence of moral absolutes, there can be no such thing as a **moral imperative**. Moral behavior might have some utility—like survival—but that wouldn't make it obligatory."

Moral imperative! More philosophy-speak. But this idea is a little easier to understand. You pose the obvious question: "How could we ever speak in terms of a 'moral imperative'—something we *must* do—unless there was a moral *authority* behind the imperative?"

Uncle is impressed with how quickly you're following the argument after such a long day of intense discussion. The sun is already starting to disappear behind the horizon.

"Moral imperatives imply a moral authority. Otherwise the 'imperative' is just an illusion. We might downgrade it to a 'suggestion' or a 'preference' but there would be no consequence for ignoring it. The knuckle-dragging proto-human could just as easily reject cooperation in favor of violent domination, and might do just as well in terms of his survival."

"Meaning that utilitarianism—did I get the word right?—can justify any choice if it achieves the desired ends?"

"Correct. And that illustrates how utilitarianism is actually moral relativism in thin disguise. You can do whatever you want and justify the action by rationalizing it with a utilitarian paint job."

"And that's because there's no way you could ever be proven wrong! You could justify even brutal behavior by the imperative of 'survival.'"

"Yes, but notice how in that context, we're describing survival as an imperative. What's wrong with that assumption?"

You see the answer right away. "Oh, wow. There can be no such thing as an imperative in a random universe!"

"So we're circling around to an answer about moral authority. If there is no Creator, there is no law."

"And no purpose. *Teleology.*" You finally got it this time.

Uncle grins. "Am I the only one in the room getting hungry?"

You grin back. "What do you like on your pizza?"

Chapter 11

Within a half hour of placing the order, the pizza arrives and Uncle graciously offers to pay for it. After some discussion, you finally decide to split the bill since he's spent the whole day helping you work through the despair of your morning walk.

As you sit at the kitchen table finishing the last of the pizza—a thin crust pepperoni with black olives from an authentic Italian restaurant—Uncle switches gears from chit-chat back to the meat of the discussion.

"When we look at the universe, what do we see? Order. Mind-boggling complexity. Beauty. Purpose. Morality. Intelligence. Information. Language. Creativity. *Love.* Is it reasonable to think these things all come from a random collision of molecules—'time and chance'?"

Now you are the one laughing out loud, almost choking on the last bite of pizza. "I would have to have an awful lot of faith to believe that!"

"Those who believe the universe came from nothing, for no reason, must indeed have a great deal of faith. Either that, or they choose to believe in a random universe because they do not want to live under the moral authority of a Creator."

"So are you saying that man rejects God for moral reasons? Don't the atheists say that God isn't necessary in order to understand how the universe came into existence?"

"Men like Dr. Richard Dawkins claim that a belief in **evolution** makes it possible to be 'an intellectually-fulfilled atheist' (as he puts it). But does it really? Is the idea of a random, purposeless, self-created universe, governed by capricious chance, an intellectually-fulfilling proposition?"

"Being 'intellectually-fulfilled' would have no meaning in a universe without purpose. Like being full of absolutely nothing." You're fairly proud of your point. "Wouldn't that be the kind of universe where we couldn't trust our own thoughts? Didn't you already make the point that without the existence of objective truth, knowledge of any kind is impossible?"

Uncle hesitates as he prepares to unleash the philosophy dictionary again. "The atheist view of the universe is referred to as **naturalistic** or **materialistic**. Similar concepts. But taking materialism, for example, the idea is that there is only material. Nothing **supernatural**. Nothing *metaphysical*. Just 'molecules in motion.' Naturalism would add that the universe is just a big machine, operating according to fixed laws of cause-and-effect."

You easily connect the dots this time. "In that kind of a universe, our thoughts are just part of the machinery."

"Correct. Materialists like Dr. Will Provine make the logical connection that free will is impossible in a mechanistic view of the universe. It's called **determinism**. Our thoughts are just electrical impulses running through the synapses of the brain, and they behave according to the same fixed laws as the stars. Hence, no free will—only an *illusion* of individual choice."

You take the additional philosophy words in stride. "Why would anybody want to believe something like that?"

"Because as we've seen, atheism is a deliberate rejection of God on *moral* grounds, not intellectual grounds. The intellectual high ground is actually on the side of a Creator. In a universe under God's authority, I not only have the capacity to think, but I can even use my thoughts and actions to glorify God."

You let the thought sink in a moment before responding. "The contrast could hardly be more striking."

"Every man faces the same choice: either give glory to the One who created you, or use the gift of creation to deliberately reject him."

"And men reject God for moral reasons." Even you're not sure if that was intended to be a question.

"As I said, atheism is not an intellectual problem, it's a moral problem. Men want to make their own rules rather than live under the authority of God."

"Which brings us back to relativism. What was the expression you used?" You're not sure if Uncle knows what you're referring to. He does.

"Radical autonomy. Except that autonomy is a myth. Everything in creation depends upon God for its existence. Everything, every moment. Autonomy is not just a myth, but it is a manifestation of absurd hubris. Man thinking that he's self-made and self-governing. Smarter than God."

"But one of the atheist's strongest criticisms of the existence of God is that our world is full of evil. How do you answer that?"

"It's an ironic criticism. Since God made man with a moral nature—the Bible says it is 'the law written on the heart'—he is able to discern the difference between good and evil. We could turn the tables and say that evil is a bigger problem for the atheist because the atheist has no way to distinguish between good and evil in an amoral universe. If there is no God, stuff just happens. So what?

There is no moral law to violate, and no reason to care about human suffering."

"But doesn't he have a point about the reality of evil?"

"He does, and the Bible explains the problem. God made man upright, but man rebelled against God and brought the curse of sin and death on the creation. We now have to live in the fallen world that *we* ruined. Assuredly, evil is real. Suffering is real. But we must understand that *man* is the one who brought evil and suffering into the world, not God."

"Do you mean to suggest that man is 'playing God' by trying to blame him for the existence of evil?"

"Man is always looking for a scapegoat in order to dodge the guilt of his own sin."

Wow. This is turning out to be theology from a fire hose, and you're struggling for air again. Uncle senses your discomfort and turns off the water for a moment. You still feel like a drowned rat.

"How about I take a quick coffee break while you let your thoughts catch up?" Staring off into the distance, you nod in agreement as Uncle steps from the dining area to the kitchen. He didn't expect a response. It was a rhetorical question.

Your thoughts continue to swirl as Uncle reheats the last cup of coffee in the microwave. You now have exactly two minutes to sort it all out. You're still amazed that anyone could believe in things likes atheism and relativism. The way Uncle explains them, they make no sense at all. In fact, they sound like rather dumb ideas.

The microwave abruptly signals the end of your mental break. You share your thoughts with Uncle as he returns to the table.

"Be careful that you differentiate between stupid people and the stupid *ideas* they latch onto. Every man is made in the image of God and has value for that reason alone—even if he rejects the truth and even if he behaves wickedly. People have a fallen nature, which means their moral and intellectual faculties have been severely damaged in the fall. The fallen mind and heart is able to hang onto all kinds of ideas that don't make sense. For most, there is little or no cognitive dissonance to warn them that something is wrong with their way of thinking."

There's that term again. Cognitive dissonance. That fog of confusion and despair that was enveloping you when Uncle knocked on the door this morning. Now you see. It was actually a warning signal to help lead you out of the fog!

"Besides," Uncle adds with a grin, "Some of the dumbest ideas turn out to be brilliant under closer examination. Like my stopping by to see you this morning."

"Point taken."

Uncle continues. "The **moral argument for the existence of God** is a compelling one. The atheist wants to use the existence of evil against the believer, but he doesn't have any way to explain evil, or even to define what it is. Differentiating good and evil requires a moral standard—which is the 'law' we've been referring to all day."

"You keep speaking as if there is only one god and one law. So what about those who argue that there are many gods, or that God is unknowable?"

"The Holy Bible is the source of God's self-revelation. He tells us everything we need to know about him—including his moral law. While the Bible is necessarily self-attesting—God can appeal to no authority higher than himself, after all—the Bible demonstrates its truth by explaining the current state of the universe, including the state of fallen man, along with the only remedy for his fallen condition. No other book is able to do this."

"But don't people disagree about what the Bible says—and what it means?"

"Arguments about what God has said and what his words mean only go back as far as the Garden of Eden," Uncle says with a sly wink. "But there are answers to the objections many people raise, in the same way we've examined many of the relativist's views in our conversation today."

"So a discussion for another day, perhaps?"

"Only if you let me buy the pizza next time."

Uncle reaches for the empty pizza box and the disposable paper plates. After depositing them in the trash, he retrieves his coffee cup from the table and motions you in the direction of the living room. The grand finale is about to begin.

Chapter 12

It's now quite dark outside and starting to get late. The soft glow of the street lamps filters through the front windows of the living room. You can tell that Uncle is bringing the discussion to a close, but he still has a few points to make. You switch on a table lamp as the two of you settle into your armchairs.

"When I knocked on your door this morning, you were sitting in this room in a state of despair. Why?"

"I guess because I left the house this morning fairly sure about my own beliefs, and by the time I circled the block I wasn't sure what to believe anymore."

Uncle pauses. There's something else. "I want you to think carefully about this next question. Are you sure that's what was bothering you? Honestly—when you made it back home, were you any *less* sure that *up is up* and *down is down*?"

You have to stop and think for a moment. After such a long day of having Uncle dissect your soul right in front of you, it's obvious that he sees something and he wants you to see it, too.

Uncle tries a slightly different angle. He's trying to help you find the answer without handing it to you. "You were in a state of despair. Perhaps resignation. But was that *really* because you didn't know what to believe anymore?"

Now you get it. Yes, that's it! "It's true that my beliefs were shaken somewhat—I mean, whose wouldn't be after hearing such an assortment of conflicting ideas? But maybe my despair was more like a case of disappointment—with myself."

Uncle leans forward and directs a stern gaze right at you. "Go on."

"Well, I felt . . . what I felt was . . . *helpless*!"

Uncle shifts forward in his seat again, urging you on without a word.

"I didn't know what to say! I'm ashamed that I didn't have a response to anyone I talked to this morning." If there was any remaining fog of despair from this morning's walk, it was now completely gone, but now you're blushing again. You realize you were falling into the pit of self-pity when Uncle knocked on the door. It was a classic case of misdiagnosing your own feelings.

"Take a deep breath." Uncle sits back. "This is probably your most important lesson all day. And I want you to realize how, with a little help, you've been teaching yourself many of these lessons."

The room is silent for what seems like several minutes before Uncle clears his throat and begins to speak again.

"I'm very proud to see how much you've learned today, and how far you've come. You've met every challenge I presented to you—including this one. *Especially* this one."

"I can't believe how blind I was to my own failure!"

"When it comes to failure, you will always be in good company. That's part of what friends are for. To help us learn things about ourselves that we can't learn as easily on our own."

As Uncle says this, you're still feeling ashamed and you reflexively scoff under your breath.

"Ah," says Uncle, as if he knows every thought, "What need have I of *your* company? Much indeed."

You're not convinced just yet.

"You may wrongly suppose that I woke up this morning magically knowing everything we've discussed today. Not so. This conversation—in a certain manner of speaking—has been many years in the making, and attended by many failures as spectacular as yours."

Somehow, that didn't help.

Now Uncle suddenly blurts out his own deepest thoughts. "You're my telos. My purpose. My mission. Whatever you may think I did for you today. . . ." Uncle has to swallow hard and clear his throat. Barely whispering, he adds, "You did . . . far more for me. It's a two-way street."

After regaining his composure, Uncle resumes his authoritative voice. "Now, you can begin to take that gift and pass it on. There are people who need to learn what you learned today."

"But. . . ."

"Be certain that you can make a difference. Never doubt it. Next time you're out for

a stroll, take time to talk. Maybe invite someone over for coffee. You never know where
that might lead."

"And what if I fail again?"

Uncle chuckles. "You will. But you'll learn
something every time. You'll get better as you
keep trying."

"And when I have questions? When I'm
stumped?"

"Put on some coffee and listen for a knock
at the door. It'll be me."

Review Questions

You may find the following questions helpful to review key ideas in the book and/or use this book for group study and discussion.

1. Think of a time when you've had to confront a view in opposition to your own. How did it challenge you regarding your own beliefs?

2. How does cognitive dissonance act as a signal that we need to examine our beliefs more carefully?

3. What are the implications of the law of noncontradiction? How can it be used to help resolve differing views?

4. Why is it so important to clarify the meaning of the words we use when we're engaged in argumentation?

5. Explain how rationality and objectivity are preconditions for epistemology.

6. Why is it necessary for science to be an ongoing process of discovery?

7. Why can't science provide answers to ethical questions?

8. Describe the difference between deontological ethics and consequentialism. Which is more difficult to apply, and why?

9. Why is it impossible to live consistently with the belief in relativism?

10. Why does the existence of moral absolutes imply a moral authority?

11. How does the materialistic view of the universe lead inevitably to a belief in determinism?

Glossary

antithetical—diametrically opposed; in philosophy, antithesis is the contrast between an idea and its opposite.

axiom—a principle that must be assumed because it cannot be proved; axioms are the building blocks for knowledge.

Big Bang—the currently prevailing cosmological paradigm that the universe originated with the explosion of a single point of matter about 15 billion years ago.

causality—the law that every effect must have an antecedent cause.

cognitive dissonance—the discomfort that results from adhering to ideas and/or actions that are in conflict with one another.

consequentialism—the branch of ethical philosophy that considers the consequences of one's moral choices.

contradiction—ideas that are in conflict in such a way that they cannot both be correct.

deontology—the branch of ethical philosophy that considers the duties that determine one's moral choices.

determinism—the belief that in a mechanistic universe, all outcomes are determined by prior conditions, including human choices. In such a system, "free will" is merely an illusion.

emotional hijacking—the point at which emotions overtake a situation and make rational analysis impossible.

epistemology—the science of knowledge.

equivocation—using a word in such a way that it has different meanings at different times in the discussion; the effect of equivocation is to draw a wrong conclusion from the argument.

evolution—the belief that life in all its present complexity arose by small changes occurring in simpler forms of life over long periods of time.

ethics—the branch of philosophy that considers the question of right and wrong.

hypothesis—an assumption about the nature of reality that is usually based on theory and/or observation and is useful for pursuing further investigation. The hypothesis is customarily assumed to be true until proven false by the available evidence.

induction—the extrapolation of specific examples to general principles; this makes it possible to draw general conclusions from small amounts of data.

law of noncontradiction—the logical law that a proposition and its opposite cannot both be true at the same time and in the same relationship.

laws of logic—a system of reasoning by reliance on axiomatic laws that make argumentation possible.

materialism (materialistic)—the belief that the universe consists only of physical matter; sometimes described as "molecules in motion."

metaphysics (metaphysical)—the branch of philosophy that addresses nonmaterial reality.

moral argument for the existence of God—the idea that without God there would be no such thing as morality; conversely, that man's moral nature points to the existence of God.

moral imperative—a moral duty, such that the failure to perform it constitutes a moral violation.

multiverse—the belief that the universe we inhabit is the one out of millions that just happens to have all the right conditions for the emergence and development of intelligent life.

naturalism (naturalistic)—the belief that the universe and everything in it is explained by the outworking of fixed natural laws.

objectivity—the idea that reality does not depend upon the observer; truth is defined by what *is*, not by what is *believed* or *perceived*.

paradox—an apparent conflict of ideas that is resolved with additional information.

philosophy—the beliefs that one holds regarding the nature of reality; worldview.

presuppositions—assumptions that come first and serve as the building blocks of knowledge.

radical autonomy—the belief that man operates without constraint from any outside influence; it explicitly rejects the moral obligations imposed on the creature by his Creator.

rationality—using one's powers of logical reasoning.

reductio ad absurdum—reducing an argument to absurdity by taking it to its logical conclusion.

relativism—the belief that truth is wholly determined by individual subjective experience.

science—the pursuit of knowledge; the study of a subject, often through experience or observation.

scientific method—a systematic approach to discovery that involves forming an hypothesis, making observations, and drawing conclusions.

self-creation—the belief that universe came into existence without the benefit of an antecedent cause.

supernatural—synonymous to *metaphysical*; that reality which exists outside the material universe.

survival of the fittest—the belief that in a complex ecosystem, survival favors the members of a species that are most well-adapted to the immediate environment; survivors then pass their selective advantages on to future generations, while the weaker members of the population die out.

syllogism—a form of reasoning consisting of premises and conclusions; analogous to an if/then statement.

teleology (telos)—the branch of philosophy that addresses meaning or purpose.

uniformity—a belief in the constancy of physical relationships across time and space; uniformity makes it possible to observe effects today and to use that knowledge to predict the same effects tomorrow.

universal—a principle that is true at all times and places.

utilitarianism—the branch of ethical philosophy that seeks to maximize the utility or preference satisfaction of those affected by our moral choices.

worldview—the beliefs that one holds regarding the nature of reality; philosophy.

Acknowledgements

Many thanks to my reviewers for a number of helpful suggestions (including the addition of the glossary and the review questions). Also thanks to those who have encouraged my long journey toward publishing a book. Success is always a team effort.

About the Author

J.R. Dickens completed a Ph.D. in mechanical engineering and enjoys writing and speaking on topics like philosophy, ethics, and Christian apologetics. He can be reached by email at jrdickens90@gmail.com.

Made in the USA
Coppell, TX
10 January 2021

47868126R00062